what we do

CONTENTS

Words in **bold** appear in the glossary on page 24.

I AM A MECHANIC

My name is Warren. I work as a mechanic in a garage. I maintain and repair all the different parts on customers' vehicles to keep them in good condition.

I work with a large variety of hand tools and power tools fixing everything from brakes, tyres and electrics to engines, gearboxes and exhaust systems.

As soon as I left school I knew I wanted to be a mechanic. I love working out how to repair cars and getting them running properly again. The most difficult part of the job is working on old cars where all the metal is **rusted** and the bolts are hard to undo.

▼ *This is the garage where I work.*

▲ *A heat gun, which burns a mixture of the gases oxygen and acetylene, can be used to loosen rusty bolts.*

There are around 31 million cars in the UK so mechanics like me are in high demand. We play a crucial role in keeping cars and people safe on the roads. We also need to have good customer service skills as we advise owners on the condition of their vehicles. Sometimes we have to give bad news if their car will be expensive to repair.

◄ *I return the keys to the customer when their car is fixed.*

KEY SKILLS

KNOWLEDGE OF MOTOR TECHNOLOGY – Mechanics require a detailed knowledge of how cars work, so it helps if you have an interest in motor vehicles.

APPRENTICESHIPS

The best way to become a car mechanic is to find a garage offering an apprenticeship programme. Apprentices train while working on the job and do some **theoretical** work at the local college each week, too.

This is Matthew (right), our apprentice. At college he is studying towards his *National Vocational Qualification (NVQ) in Vehicle Maintenance and Repair*. In the garage he **shadows** Dave, our senior mechanic, to learn some of the more complicated jobs.

▼ *Dave shows Matthew how to replace a brake pipe.*

▲ *Taking a wheel off and putting it back on is a simple job for an apprentice.*

At the start of an apprenticeship you will sweep and tidy the workshop, make drinks and watch the other mechanics at work. Then you will start to do basic jobs yourself, such as fitting tyres or replacing brake pads.

You do not have to have any specific qualifications to become an apprentice, but employees usually want someone who has good GCSE results in Maths, English, Science and Design Technology.

KEY SKILLS

ABILITY TO FOLLOW INSTRUCTIONS – To learn methods you need to listen to instructions and carry them out.

Any experience that shows you have practical skills will also give you a real advantage. Big car companies, such as BMW and Honda recruit apprentices every year. My tip is to ask your local garages first because mechanics' jobs are not always advertised.

TESTING VEHICLES

By law, every car in the UK over three years old has to pass an annual **MOT** test to prove that it is safe to drive. To carry out MOT tests, mechanics must have experience and extra training.

Dave is our MOT tester. He checks the key pieces of equipment on the cars, such as the windscreen wipers (below), lights, tyres and mirrors. Using computerised equipment he also tests the car's exhaust. He has to check that the car is not producing too many harmful gases.

▲ *When Dave operates the rear lights he uses a mirror to check that they are working.*

KEY SKILLS

ATTENTION TO DETAIL –
You must be able to spot faults
so that cars are repaired properly
and are safe to drive.

To check that the brakes
are in good condition
Dave drives the wheels
of the car on to a set of
rolling pipes (right).
He then presses down
on the brake and uses
a remote control to
operate a computer
nearby. The computer
gives a reading that
shows if the brakes
are worn or not.

TOOLS OF THE TRADE

Using the **hydraulic** ramp,
Dave does further tests
on the car. To check the
suspension, the wheels
are placed on metal
plates which wobble and
shake when you press a
switch. Dave then lifts
the car with a **jack** and
spins the wheels so he
can hear if the **bearings**
need replacing (left).

If Dave finds any faults he fails the
car and writes down the repair work
needed. After the repairs are done he
has to retest the car. Once it passes he
prints off an MOT certificate for the
customer (right).

SERVICE TIME

Customers often bring their cars to the garage for a **service**. At a service I run checks and do maintenance work on the vehicle. The work I do keeps cars in good condition, and can prevent them breaking down in the future.

During a service I complete a checklist. I check the car over visually and make sure that major parts, such as the brakes and tyres are not worn. The brakes are also cleaned and adjusted. Then I replace the oil, screenwash and the **filters**.

▲ *I pour the screenwash into the windscreen washer tank.*

▲ *On my job sheet I write down the work I have done and note any extra work that I think is needed.*

KEY SKILLS

ABILITY TO WORK ON YOUR OWN – You should be able to work independently without **supervision**, but you should also be willing to work as part of a team.

Here, Matthew is changing the engine oil (right). To remove the old oil he unbolts the covering underneath the car and lets the oil spill out into an oil drainer.

After a car has been driven so many miles, certain parts should be replaced. This car (below right) has done 80,000 miles, so I am taking the **spark plugs** out of the engine and replacing them. At the end of a service I give the car a quick road test to check everything is working properly.

▼ *Changing the spark plugs is a common job during a service.*

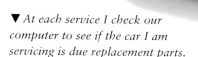

▼ *At each service I check our computer to see if the car I am servicing is due replacement parts.*

IDENTIFYING FAULTS

If a customer brings in a car that is malfunctioning we have to find out what the problem is, so it can be fixed. Some faults are obvious while others are hard to identify.

I listen carefully to the customer as they describe the trouble they are having with their vehicle. Then I run tests to confirm a fault. I sometimes go out with the customer in their car so they can show me what is wrong.

▼ *A flat tyre like this one is easy to spot, but some problems require more investigation.*

If the car is making a strange noise, we often raise the car on the ramp to inspect it underneath. We check parts such as the suspension and steering joints for a **mechanical** fault. Depending on the fault we repair a part or replace it completely.

I also use electrical equipment to find faults. If an error light shows up on the car's **dashboard** I plug a **diagnostic machine** into the car and run some tests.

▲ *Here, Dave is using a torch to inspect the underneath of the car.*

▶ *The diagnostic machine can pinpoint faults on many different makes of vehicle.*

FITTING PARTS

When mechanics replace parts we often have to take sections of the car to bits. Once the new part is put in place we must put everything back together correctly.

When we fit a new clutch (below left), first we have to take out the front wheels, suspension, gearbox and all of the connecting rods and shafts. To remove the large nuts and bolts that hold parts together we use **air guns** like this one (below).

▲ *A clutch connects the engine to the gearbox.*

▲ *As Dave fits the new clutch, a jack is put in place to hold the engine up and stop it falling out.*

▲ *The power in an air gun comes from* **compressed** *air that is suddenly released.*

KEY SKILLS

STRENGTH AND FITNESS – Lifting heavy parts such as engines and gearboxes is physically demanding.

▲ *In tight spaces I use a socket wrench to turn nuts and bolts.*

Some jobs are simple, such as attaching a new wiper blade (left). Attaching a whole new wiper arm under the bonnet is not so easy (above). We have some of the new parts in stock in the garage. For other items I have to phone up the parts shop down the road and order them in.

▼ *The local parts shop delivers the tools and parts I have ordered.*

REPAIR WORK

We need to be skilled with a variety of tools when we carry out repairs. We must also keep up to date with the latest technology, such as new engines and electronics, so we can fix things.

To fix a car with a hole in its side I cut a piece of steel to size with the snips (right). I hold the steel in place with some **mole grips** and then I **weld** the new metal to the surface of the car with extreme heat (below).

▼ *The heat fuses the new metal to the old metal and covers up the hole.*

KEY SKILLS

PATIENCE – Finding faults and repairing them can take time. You must be patient and make sure you do the whole job well.

As I weld the metal, it bubbles up. I hammer the bubbles down and flatten them off with another power tool called a grinder (right). I then spray a black **sealant** on, to protect the metal.

Repairing faults has to be done carefully and accurately. It is vital that the car is returned to the customer in a safe condition.

TOOLS OF THE TRADE

After a car's suspension is repaired, I check that the wheels are lined up perfectly with a laser machine (below). The machine has clamps which fasten to each wheel and the steering wheel.

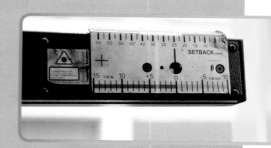

Lasers from the machine shine on to gauges on the inside of the clamps (above) and tell me if any of the wheels need adjusting.

▶ *I must fasten the clamps to each wheel to get an accurate reading from the laser.*

TYRE CHANGES

Replacing or repairing damaged tyres is one of the most common jobs for a car mechanic. If the tyre's **tread** has worn down to less than 1.6 millimetres, by law it must be replaced.

I operate a tyre changing machine to remove the tyre from the wheel, and put the new tyre on. Sometimes I use a pry bar to help lever the tyre on and off, too. Then I inflate the tyre to the correct pressure.

▲ *A pry bar has a flat end to force the tyre and wheel apart.*

▲▼ *I use a gauge to measure the depth of a tyre's tread.*

▶ *I grease up a tyre with tyre soap so it can be pushed back on more easily.*

If the tyre is punctured it can be repaired as long as the damage is not too close to the side wall. We clamp the tyre to the table and drill the hole bigger (right). Then we glue a patch over the hole and smooth the patch down with a power tool.

When a new tyre is fitted we use a machine to check that the wheel is balanced. If the weight of the wheel is uneven we clip a metal weight on to one side of the wheel's rim so that the weight becomes even.

◄ *Before I put the wheel back on the car, I balance the weight of it.*

KEY SKILLS

DEXTERITY – Mechanics should be able to work skilfully with their hands.

WORKING CONDITIONS

My regular working hours are 8am to 5pm from Monday to Friday. Occasionally I work an extra shift on a Saturday morning. Mechanics who work for a breakdown service may be called out in the middle of the night.

At a breakdown a mechanic has to work in all types of weather. Even in our garage it gets really cold and draughty in winter. It is also very messy working with oil and grease. I use **latex** gloves so that I am not constantly having to scrub oil from my skin. Some people rub a barrier cream into their skin to prevent them getting rashes.

◄ *Replacing a shock absorber is a messy job.*

The job is physically hard. Some parts that we repair require us to work in awkward and uncomfortable positions. We also have to handle heavy and dangerous parts. We are trained in health and safety to make us aware of the risks.

◄ *Heavy parts have to be lifted properly so that we don't get injured.*

▼ *The brightness produced during welding can seriously damage your eyes if you do not wear a mask.*

You have to be very sensible when you are working with power tools. Sometimes I wear goggles to protect my eyes. When I weld, I wear a face mask to shield my eyes from the bright light.

KEY SKILLS

CONCENTRATION – On a long job you need to keep your focus. A moment's loss of concentration can be dangerous.

GETTING ON

If you cannot find an apprenticeship you can take your mechanic qualifications first. The *City and Guilds Certificate in Vehicle Maintenance and Repair* or the *BTEC National Certificate in Vehicle Repair and Technology* are offered by a wide range of colleges.

■ There are plenty of opportunities for qualified mechanics. As well as garages, jobs can be found with breakdown services and places that have a **fleet** of vehicles, such as taxi companies, vehicle hire firms or the police.

■ Experienced mechanics who have gained a knowledge of how business works often go into management or choose to set up their own garage. This can be very **lucrative**.

▶ *This is my manager Colin, who runs the garage.*

As a mechanic it is important that we continually update and improve our skills. You can train to be an MOT tester and take a qualification that will allow you to service a car's air conditioning unit. There is also the chance to focus on one particular area of mechanics, such as tyres, electrics or bodywork repair.

Mechanics who like a different challenge can join the army, working on armoured vehicles, or even become a racing car engineer. A Formula 1 victory is down to the mechanics' hard work as well as the driver's.

▼ Racing car engineers need to pay great attention to detail, because the cars they work on have to be set up perfectly for the race.

◄ This certificate shows that I am qualified to fix a car's air conditioning.

KEY SKILLS

AMBITION AND PASSION – You need to be enthusiastic about cars and have a determination to succeed.

GLOSSARY

air gun A tool which uses compressed air.

bearing A part of a car that allows the wheel to spin smoothly with very little friction.

compressed Squeezed or pushed into a smaller space.

dashboard The panel facing the driver of a vehicle which contains instruments and controls.

diagnostic machine A tool used to find out what is causing a car to malfunction.

filter A device that removes unwanted particles from a liquid or gas. On a car there is an air, fuel and oil filter.

fleet A number of vehicles owned by the same person or organization.

hydraulic Power that comes from pushing liquid through a tube.

jack A piece of equipment for lifting a car so that the wheel can be inspected and changed.

latex A rubber made from the milky fluid found in many plants.

lucrative Producing a lot of profit.

mechanical To do with machinery.

mole grip A tool that holds something in position with a pair of locking jaws.

MOT MOT stands for Ministry of Transport, a department of government which introduced the car safety test.

rusted Rusted iron and steel turns brown and flaky. It forms when the metal is exposed to air and water.

sealant A material used to seal and protect something from the air and water.

service A regular inspection and set of adjustments to keep a vehicle working well.

shadow Follow someone and watch them closely.

spark plug An electrical device which starts the fuel burning in an engine.

supervision Direction and observation to make sure someone carries out a task properly.

theoretical Based on the ideas behind a subject rather than the practical skills.

tread The ridges on a tyre to prevent it slipping.

weld Join together by heating the surfaces to the point of melting.

INDEX

This edition published in 2014 by

Franklin Watts
338 Euston Road
London NW1 3BH

Franklin Watts Australia
Level 17/207 Kent Street
Sydney, NSW 2000

Planning and production by
Discovery Books Limited
Editor: James Nixon
Design: sprout.uk.com
Commissioned photography: Bobby Humphrey

Dewey number: 629.2'87

ISBN: 978 1 4451 2947 1

Printed in China

Franklin Watts is a division of Hachette
Children's Books, an Hachette UK company.

www.hachette.co.uk

Acknowledgements: Shutterstock Images: p. 23
bottom (mypokcik).

The author, packager and publisher would like
to thank Bankside Garage, Leeds, for their help
and participation in this book.

what we do

Mechanic

JAMES NIXON

PHOTOGRAPHY BY BOBBY HUMPHREY